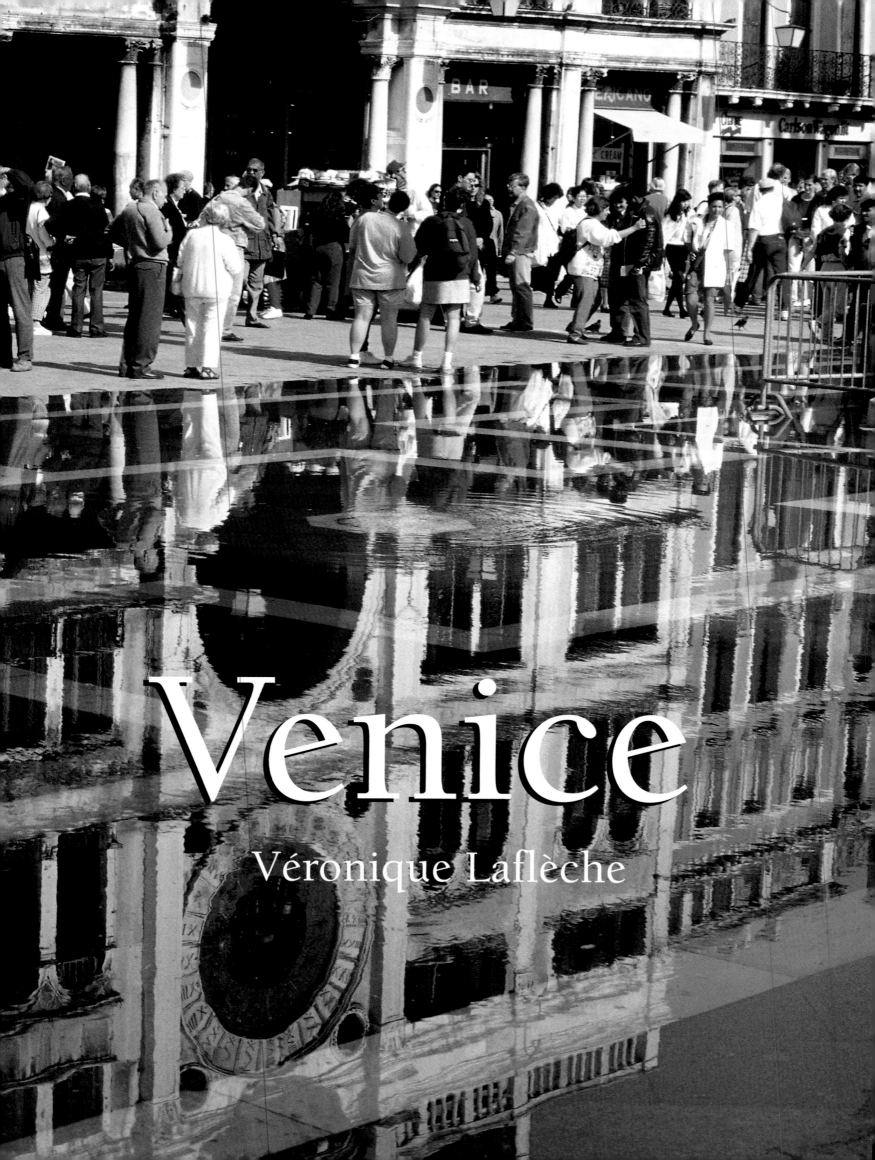

Venice

Véronique Laflèche

INTRODUCTION

NOWHERE else in the world is like Venice, a city that seems to have emerged out of the water as if by magic.

Subject through the ages to many different architectural influences – Byzantine, Gothic, Renaissance and Baroque – the city today displays nothing but perfect harmony in form and style. The visitor, within the distance of an easy walk, can marvel at the Grand Canal and its sumptuous palaces, gaze in rapt admiration at magnificent Venetian paintings, and may even hear music coming from the odd corner.

Yes, Venice may be something of a museum piece in its own right, but it is also very much a real, live, working city. It has its university, its Rialto market, its *campi*. It is both quietly elegant and boisterously popular.

HISTORY

URING the time of the Roman Empire, the area that now corresponds to most of the province of Venezia was inhabited by the people whom the Romans called the Veneti. Their territory centred on the lagoon – then an unprepossessing, not to say unhealthy, swamp on the Adriatic coast between Trieste and Ravenna – where they occupied flimsy shacks made of reed-stems that were sited either on the *barene* (the sandbanks) or on the islands. They made a meagre living by fishing and by producing and trading in salt.

Then in 697 the combined inhabitants of the lagoon area, technically under the suzerainty of Byzantium, decided to elect a leader for themselves. He was to be their *doge* (a title cognate with Latin *dux*, English *duke*). To begin with, the doge's seat of power was Malamocco, but it rapidly became necessary to transfer to Rialto, which was less exposed to enemy incursions. And when that happened, in 810, many of the inhabitants of the little islands dotted all about the lagoon seized the opportunity to move there too.

Now it was the custom in that age for towns and cities to regard themselves as under the individual patronage and protection of a saint, whose relics each cherished in its major church. The Byzantine saint Theodore was the contemporary patron-protector of Rialto and the lagoon. However, two merchants from Venice trading in Alexandria took it upon themselves to 'acquire' relics of the body of St Mark the Evangelist there, and to return with the bones to Rialto. The men arrived back in the year of 828, and placed the relics in the charge of the Doge, then Giustiniano Partecipazio. Delighted, the

1. The Piazza inundated by the *acqua alta*
2. View of San Marco across the Bacino San Marco
3. Giovanni Bellini (Giambellino), *Doge Leonardo Loredan*, 1501–1505, oil on canvas, 61,5 x 45 cm, National Gallery, London
4. Guardi, *The Bacino San Marco with San Giorgio Maggiore and the Giudecca*, 1774?,oil on canvas, 72 x 97 cm, Accademia, Venice

7

Doge decided at once to have a ducal chapel built alongside his official residence – and St Mark, whose symbol, the winged lion, may be seen throughout the city, thus for ever replaced St Theodore.

Between 800 and 1000 the city endeavoured to detach itself altogether from Byzantium, and to begin to establish its own empire. The only direction in which this was possible was seawards, which and that being the case, the lack of security in the Adriatic was the first problem that had to be dealt with. So it came to pass that in the year 1000, with the help of the Byzantines, the Doge – Pietro Orseolo II – led a punitive expedition against the coast-dwellers of Dalmatia and won a resounding victory. Venice became ruler of the high seas. Every year since then, on Ascension Day (*la Festa della Sensa*), the city has celebrated its 'marriage' to the waters.

The city at that point took the name of its original inhabitants, the Veneti – in modern English, Venice, but the citizens are *Venetians* even now.

In 1204 it was the contemporary Doge of Venice, old Enrico Dandolo, who organised the Fourth Crusade – a venture that led to the capture of Constantinople, which was then sacked. The Byzantine Empire had been brought to its knees, and in the process Venice was enriched by the astounding amount of booty that found its way back there.

Following the Fourth Crusade, the city came into possession of territories all around the Mediterranean Basin. Merchant ships from many countries travelled in convoys under the protection of escorting Venetian galleons armed to the teeth against the depradations of pirates and Turkish raiders. Such trade reached its peak during the 13th and 14th centuries, and in turn gave rise to something else that added to the city's great good fortune. In 1284 Venice struck its own coinage, the ducat (*ducato*, because it bore the effigy of the *duca* or Doge), which was to become the standard currency of trade over the whole of the eastern Mediterranean.

There were setbacks, however. Venice suffered a series of virulent plagues (including the Black Death) which decimated its population and affected its ability to wage war on its great maritime rival, Genoa, for mastery of the high seas.

In 1453, the Ottoman Turks seized Constantinople, which was thereafter known as Istanbul. The Byzantine Empire no longer existed. Diplomatic arrangements had to be made so that Venice might continue its commercial enterprises. Accordingly, Venice signed a peace treaty with the Ottoman leaders in 1479 in an exchange deal by which the city agreed to give up several Greek islands and to pay 'compensation', in return for being allowed to make use of the island of Cyprus as a valuable trade base in the eastern Mediterranean. This was possible only because a Venetian lady, Caterina Corner, had married the king of Cyprus and in due course had been widowed but had held on to the reins of power there.

It was in the second half of the 16th century that certain wealthy Venetians experiencing commercial difficulties turned their attention away from maritime

trade and built themselves some large, comfortable and well-appointed houses out in the countryside inland.

During much of the 18th century the resources of Venice were stretched to the limit both by incessant wars against the Turks and by recurrent epidemics of the plague. In a heart-felt desire to find peace the city turned in on itself. Venetians abandoned themselves to hedonistic pleasures, to enjoying each day for as long as it lasted. This is the Baroque Venice of Casanova, Goldoni, Vivaldi, Tiepolo...

And it was in this somewhat decadent context that its last Doge, Ludovico Manin, on 12 May 1797 abdicated in favour of Napoleon Bonaparte. The city thereafter fell under Austrian sway (1814–66) until it was included within the Kingdom of Italy following a plebiscite (1866).

Venice joined itself once and for all to the mainland in 1846, when a railway causeway was constructed. A new harbour was built at around the same time. Then

5

the Accademia and Stazione bridges were added. Thoroughfares were created, cutting through to link up Santa Lucia station with the city centre.

Yet in comparison with the shining enthusiasm of Venice in the 18th century, the 19th century featured nothing but misery. By 1820 fewer than 100,000 residents lived in the city, and were subject to abject poverty. And in the 20th century – perhaps the greatest misfortune of all to the Laguna Veneta – an industrial zone of considerable magnitude was established at Porto Marghera and Mestre. The road and rail links were doubled in size (via the Ponte della Liberté in 1933). Marco Polo airport was opened in 1961.

The great flood (*acqua alta*) of 4 November 1966 and the La Fenice fire of 29 January 1996 dismayed not only the Venetians but the whole world. The events served to awaken people everywhere to what might happen if nothing was done, to react accordingly, to make funds available at once, and to do all that was necessary to try to rescue this unique city.

VENICE TODAY

Venice is sliced in two by the Grand Canal (*Canal Grande*). Altogether, the city comprises 118 little islands separated from each other by a multitude of small canals (some 160 in all) called *rii*. The original inhabitants used to go from place to place by boat. Then, to make life a little easier, bridges were built to link islands to each other. Today, the number of bridges is up around the 400 mark – and to save themselves from even the least particle of wasted energy, many Venetians willingly choose a slightly longer route so long as there are fewer bridges to cross.

Inside the city there is water everywhere. In addition to the canals, the great number of well-heads bear witness to the concern of the citizens always to have their own supply of drinking water. But water flows outside the city too, for Venice is itself situated in the middle of a lagoon in which sea water is trapped between the solid mainland and an almost (but not quite) continuous offshore strip or belt, called the *lido*. To a great extent Venice is protected from the Adriatic by this natural coastal belt actually comprising three *lidi* – from north to south the Lido di Iesolo, the Lido di Venezia (generally known simply as the Lido) and the Lido di Pellestrina – separated by three gaps (the Porto di Lido, the Porto di Malamocco and the Porto di Chioggia).

Every visitor arriving in Venice for the first time is caught by surprise by this 'city in the water'. The usual form of public transport is water-borne, by *vaporetto* or *motoscafo*, as is the transportation in the city of all kinds of merchandise, even household removals. Only the emergency services are authorised to exceed the speed restriction on the water .

The other way to travel round the city is to go on foot down the narrow alleys called *calli* or to walk to

5. The church of Santa Maria della Salute, seen from the Accademia

9

the main shopping streets (*rughe*), perhaps on streets alongside the canals (*fondamente*), to emerge on the squares (*campi*, and the smaller *campielli*), maybe crossing a few bridges on the way, to saunter down a side-street (*ramo*) or two – some of which are dead-ends – or even to venture down a covered way (*sottoportego*). It is not possible to get lost in Venice. Signs and maps enable the tourist always to find the way. At worst, a genial Venetian will with much waving of arms tell the bemused tourist to 'go in that direction and keep straight on'! Theoretically, that is all that is ever required –

although of course in Venice there is never actually a 'straight on' to go.

One of the first things to strike the first-time tourist is the lack of cars and trucks and all the noises that go with them in any other city. Yes, there are the sounds of the *vaporetti*, the lapping and splashing of the water, the occasional animated argument on the streets, and the footsteps. But such sounds are never continuous, are always changing from moment to moment, day and night, and they are all comparatively muted. When the Venetians decide to sleep in of a morning, the city remains deserted. The water in the canals is dark and black, and at the slightest hint of sea-mist the city takes on an aspect of ghostly unreality. This might seem rather worrying, and yet Venice is one of the safest places of all to be.

Every season has its own colour. The winter is seen through a cold, crystalline light. The summer is cloaked in a veil of humid heat. Certainly, in some respects Venice is all things to all people in a mystical sort of way, but it is genuinely possible for anyone and everyone who goes there to pick out something that is delightful, and that appeals to the emotions.

One thing is for sure: Venice is the city in which the greatest number of riches and works of beauty are crammed into the most restricted space. There is also something peculiar about the sense of time. Time doesn't seem to pass at the same rate in Venice as it does in other cities. Everything is slower – maybe at walking speed. To live in Venice is to learn to be patient.

6. A well-head on the Campo San Marcuola
7. The Ponte delle Pazienze

SAN MARCO

SAN MARCO is the district of Venice most visited by tourists, and is the true historical centre of the city. It includes the Doge's Palace (Palazzo Ducale), the seat of the political and judiciary power; the basilica of San Marco (St Mark's), the seat of the spiritual power; and the Rialto, seat of the economic power.

A visitor arriving from the open sea, having entered into the lagoon through one of the gaps in the offshore strip, finds himself or herself in the Bacino San Marco and is all of a sudden surrounded by beauty and magnificence. Disembarking on the Molo (the quayside by San Marco), the visitor's eye is caught by two towering pillars. To the right is the pillar of St Mark, with its winged lion in bronze. To the left is the pillar of St Theodore, first patron saint of Venice.

The original Doge's Palace, built in 814, looked like a fortified Byzantine citadel. Many times burned down, it was reconstructed and finally completed in the 16th century in a flamboyant gothic style evidently still derived from Byzantine inspiration. It remains an impressive building covered in diamond-chequered tilework in pink and white marble, the arched colonnades lending the construction an aspect of lightness and elegance.

8. The Doge's Palace and the Bell-Tower (*Campanile*)

The main entrance to the Palace is through the Porta della Carta, above which Doge Foscari is depicted kneeling before the winged lion of St Mark. The hall inside contains the Giants' Staircase, with the statues of Mars and Neptune by Jacopo Sansovino (commissioned 1554), leading to the first floor where the Doge had his apartments. The Grand Council Chamber, the largest room in the Palace, is festooned with murals by Veronese, by Giovane Palma ('Young' Palma) and by da Bassano. On the back wall is one of the greatest masterpieces in the world, Tintoretto's *Paradise* (1590). It is in this chamber that official receptions are held.

Access to the second floor is by the Golden Staircase completed in 1559. The legislative and executive authorities occupy the Senate Chamber, and the magistrates hold their conventions in the College Room, in which Veronese's *Battle of Lepanto* is on exhibition.

The famous prison cells are located within the roof space (the Leads) or at ground level (the Wells). From the former, one notable escapee in 1756 was a certain Giacomo Casanova… Access to the New Prison, built in

the 16th century, is via the Bridge of Sighs which links to the Rio di Palazzo. This is where the last sighs of those condemned to execution were to be heard…

Joined to the Doge's Palace, the splendid basilica of San Marco faces full-on to the Piazza in front of it. Like the Doge's Palace, the basilica has in its time undergone a series of major fires. Constructed in the overall shape of a Greek cross and surmounted by five cupolas, it follows the plan of Hagia Sophia in Istanbul/Constantinople and harmoniously combines elements of Byzantine, Islamic, Roman, Gothic and even Renaissance styles.

9. The riva degli Schiavoni
10. The Doge's Palace and the St Mark pillar

On the outside of the basilica, the left-hand portal is decorated with mosaics illustrating the translation of the body of St Mark (13th century). Above the central portal, on the outer loggia, is a copy of The Four Horses in gilded bronze. The original was yet another piece removed from Constantinople, but was then 'borrowed' for some years by Napoleon Bonaparte. Today it is housed in the basilica's museum. To the right of the basilica stands a sculpture in red porphyry representing The Tetrarchs (4th century).

The interior of St Mark's is bathed in a golden light. Superb mosaics on a golden ground, completed over the course of several centuries, cover the walls, the pillars and the cupolas to an astonishing total of more than 4,000 square metres (43,000 square feet), illustrating scenes from the Bible.

Coming back to earth, the floor is a mosaic pavement of marble tessarae in a multitude of colours. In the choir, the Pala d'Oro or golden retable was completed in the 14th century by a Venetian goldsmith. It is made up of a large number of enamelled gold plaques and thousands of precious stones – items 'acquired' in combat on the Mediterranean high seas.

11. The Giants' Stairs: Sansovino's statues of Mars and Neptune
12. The interior courtyard of the Doge's Palace

The Piazetta, the old harbour basin built up in the 12th century, is located between the Doge's Palace on the one hand and the archaeological museum and the Marciana Library on the other. It extends as far as the Molo. On the Piazetta, the Campanile (the Bell-Tower) was erected between the 9th century and the 16th, but then collapsed on 14 July 1902 to become no more than a shapeless heap of rubble. It was restored in 1912 *dov' era e com' era* ('where it was and as it was').

The Marciana Library (Libreria Vecchia di San Marco), constructed 1537–53, is another masterpiece by Sansovino. One of the richest collections of ancient books in Italy, it was also a significant beneficiary of the capture of Constantinople in 1453 and of the printing press established in Venice during the 16th century.

From the end of the Piazetta, on the Molo, a magnificent view extends over the Bacino San Marco, the Giudecca and San Giorgio.

The Piazza – the only one to be so called in Venice – is the largest square in the city. In the 11th century it was a cottage garden crossed by a canal. Not actually square but trapezoidal, its shape dates from the beginning of the 12th century. The original brick paving (1267) was replaced in 1723 with flagstones.

Each side of the Piazza, the Procuratie Vecchie and the Procuratie Nuove now house civil servants. And the celebrated Café Florian and Café Quadri continue to attract tourists in droves.

It was Napoleon who decided to make the Piazza an enclosed space. Accordingly, in 1807 he had the church of San Geminiano demolished (although it had been designed again by Sansovino) and in its place constructed the Procuratie Nuovissime. The 'Napoleon wing' is now occupied by the Correr museum of daily life in the history of Venice. Among the museum's exhibits are sculptures by Canova.

13. The Bridge of Sighs
14. Cupolas on the basilica of San Marco

15–16. Inside the basilica of San Marco
17. Mosaics illustrating Biblical texts
18. The Four Horses in gilded bronze

At one end of the Procuratie Vecchie, where the main shopping streets (*mercerie*) begin, the Clock-Tower (Torre dell' Orologio) of Mauro Codussi, completed in the 15th century, features an attractively bold blue dial. On its front is the winged lion of St Mark, and at the top two costumed Moors strike the hour.

The Piazza is the lowest point in the entire city of Venice, and not unnaturally is completely flooded several times a year by the tide. On 4 November 1966, a particularly high tide (*acqua alta*) inundated the square to a depth of very nearly 4 feet (1.2 metres).

In order to get to the Rialto Bridge, the shortest way requires going down several of the main shopping streets (*mercerie*). Another possibility is to go to the bottom of the square and make towards the Campo San Moise, and from there towards the Campo San Maurizio. Here are the expensive shops – the jewellers and of course the couturiers and dress shops such as Fortuny and Rubelli.

On the Campo San Fantin, the Fenice Theatre was renowned during the 19th and for most of the 20th century for its operatic productions. While renovation work was being carried out in January 1996, however, an electrical fault caused the place to burn down. It rose again from its own ashes, like the phoenix after which it had been named, and within two years was rebuilt. To this day, though, it remains shrouded from view within huge sheets of cloth.

To get from the Piazza to the Ponte dell' Accademia means going through either the Campo San Stefano or the Campo Francesco Morosini. From there, different *campi* lead to the Campo San Bartolomeo, which is not far from the Rialto Bridge.

Off to one side of the Campo Manin is the Palazzo Contarini del Bovolo, built in Byzantine-gothic and Renaissance styles. It has a spiral staircase up the outside.

On the Campo San Beneto is the Gothic Palazzo Pesaro degli Orfei, rebuilt by Mariano Fortuny (renowned for his famous plissées silks). Today the Palazzo houses the Fortuny Museum.

18

21

19. Inside the basilica of San Marco

23. Gondolas in the the Bacino San Marco
24. Campo San Stefano
25. The spiral staircase outside the Palazzo Contarini del Bovolo

DORSODURO

COMING from San Marco, cross the Grand Canal by ferry (*traghetto*) at the cost of several hundred lire, go as far as the Campo del Traghetto, and you will be close to the Salute. Alternatively, walk across the Ponte dell'Accademia which links San Marco and Dorsoduro. This is where an iron bridge was set up during the Austrian occupation (mid-19th century) that was destroyed in 1930. A temporary wooden bridge then replaced it. In every direction from the highest point on the bridge – finally rebuilt in 1985 – there are tremendous views of *palazzi*.

At the foot of the Ponte dell' Accademia, on the Campo della Carità, stands the Accademia Museum, now occupying the site of the former Scuola Granda della Carità (the Grand Charity Guildhall), its church and its monastery. Opened in 1817, the museum contains an excellent collection of Venetian paintings from between the 14th and 18th centuries.

Fourteenth-century 'primitive' painters (such as Paolo and Lorenzo Veneziano) were swayed by Byzantine and Gothic influences. In the 15th century, painting became more realistic (as in the works of del Fiori, Vivarini and the Bellinis). It was Jacopo Bellini who established Italian Gothic, and one of his sons, Gentile, who took over his father's studio and worked particularly on portraits. Jacopo also executed paintings for the *scuole*, among which is the remarkable *Procession From St Mark's Square* (1496). Jacopo's other son, Giovanni, became famous for his madonnas.

Like Gentile Bellini, Vittorio Carpaccio depicted scenes of ordinary everyday life in Venice. *The Curing of the Man Possessed* actually shows the very old Rialto Bridge, the wooden one which was high enough at the centre to allow boats to pass beneath without having to take down their masts. His *Scenes From the Life of St Ursula* is full of bits and pieces characteristic of the period.

26. The Salute and the Punta della Dogana, seen from the Giudecca

Venetian art of the 17th century may not have been anything like so fascinating, but the 18th century gave the city its last truly great painters during a time of feasts and spectacles... and despite a remorseless economic recession and a dearth of artistic patrons.

Canaletto, Longhi and Guardi all painted *vedute* – paintings that were 'views' of Venice and that contained scenes of everyday life. As for the towering Tiepolo, no one could have expected him to create veritable masterpieces in a Venice on the verge of collapse. Abandoning the shades and shadows of Tintoretto, he borrowed the colours of Veronese, with the result that his paintings and frescoes have a wonderful sense of light and of lightness.

Before leaving the Accademia, the visitor should look closely at the floor, the surface of which is made up of tiny tiles to which oil has been applied so that they don't break. This type of semi-flexible flooring – *terrazzo alla veneziana* – was invented to provide extra stability on an insecure base, particularly in the event of earth-tremors.

Not far from the Accademia Museum, but further down the Grand Canal towards the Bacino San Marco, is a *palazzo* only a single storey high. This is the Palazzo Venier dei Leoni built for the Venier family. Construction on it began in 1749, but the building was never completed and no one now knows why not. In 1949, the American Peggy Guggenheim bought it and filled it with contemporary paintings and sculptures. Her diligence has resulted in what is currently the most important private collection of modern art in Europe, containing works by Picasso, Ernst (whom she married), Pollock, de Chirico, Chagall, Magritte, Man Ray and others.

In the 16th century, Giorgione's *The Tempest* – painted in 1507 – marked him out as distinct from contemporary 'primitive' painters. The Venetian painter Lorenzo Lotto likewise bequeathed to posterity an admirable *Portrait of a Gentleman of Leisure* (1525). But it was Titian who really dominated painting during the 16th century. He was not concerned if he painted great religious or mythological compositions or if he executed portraits of the great and good of his time. *Pietà*, a sombre piece originally intended to ornament his own tomb, turned out in fact to be the last work he did, for he died of the plague in August 1576 when it was still incomplete. Tintoretto, a painter inspired by religion, painted *The Creation of the Animals*, a masterpiece full of movement. And finally, the greatest colorist of the 16th century can be no one else but Veronese, who worked so incredibly hard to decorate the Doge's Palace. A light-hearted painter who enjoyed wealth, Veronese is well known for his *Battle of Lepanto*. But it was his *The Meal at the House of Levi* (1576), commissioned by the Dominicans of Santi Giovanni e Paolo, that got him into serious trouble with the religious authorities of the Inquisition because they considered the work too profane in style. He retrieved the situation without too much trouble: he changed the title to *The Lord's Supper*.

29

27. Titian: *Pietà*, 1576, oil on canvas, 378 x 374 cm, Accademia,
    Venice
28. The Accademia
29. Vittorio Carpaccio: *Scenes From the Cross: The Miracle of the Cross at
    Rialto Bridge, The Curing of a Man Possessed*, 1494, oil on canvas,
    363 x 406 cm, Accademia, Venice

Towards the tip of Dorsoduro stands the imposing church of Santa Maria della Salute, built by Baldassare Longhena as a gesture of gratitude to the Virgin Mary for having brought an end to the terrible epidemic of plague that seized Venice in 1630. In baroque style, octagonal in shape and surmounted by a large cupola, it is graced by statues of the Twelve Apostles in white Istrian stone. To support the building, more than a million wooden piles were driven into the soil beneath.

The interior of the Salute is somewhat bleak, despite the beautiful mosaic pavement. Works of art by Giordano, by Titian and by Tintoretto (*The Wedding at*

30

Cana) add some warmth and personality to this enormous church.

The very tip of Dorsoduro, Punta della Dogana (Customs Point), affords a view that is simply not possible from the Piazzetta of the Doge's Palace, the Riva degli Schiavoni (the foreshore of the Bacino San Marco) and the islands of San Giorgio and the Giudecca. On the seaward side of the Punta, the Dogana di Mare – a complex of buildings restored at the end of the 17th century – was intended to regulate the arrival of all seagoing vessels in Venice.

From there, the visitor can amble along the southern side of Dorsoduro, looking from the Fondamente Zattere across the wide Canale della Giudecca (in which *canale* this time means 'channel'). Also on the Fondamente Zattere are many of the old warehouses used for the salt trade back in the 14th century, though reconstructed during the 19th. The church of the Gesuati, dating from the 18th century, contains one or two works by Tiepolo.

The workshop at which gondolas are made and repaired is located by the Campo San Trovaso. And a little further west still, the church of San Sebastiano, built in the 16th century, is one of those decorated by Veronese.

But coming back in towards the centre of Dorsoduro, the ambling tourist may instead visit the church of Santa Maria del Carmelo or dei Carmini, built at the end of the 13th century, although its brick façade dates from the 16th. Inside are paintings by Lorenzo Lotto, by Cima da Conegliano and by Ricci. Beside it is the Scuola Grande dei Carmini, the last building in the city to be decorated in rococo style. On its ceiling, the frescoes by Tiepolo date from the 18th century, and the monochrome paintings are by Piranesi.

30. Giorgione: *The Tempest*, 1510, oil on canvas, 82 x 73 cm, Accademia, Venice
31. Veronese: *The Meal at the House of Levi* (detail), oil on canvas, 555 x 1,310 cm, 1573?, Accademia, Venice
32. Tintoretto: *The Creation of the Animals*, oil on canvas, 151 x 258 cm, 1550?, Accademia, Venice

31

32

33. Gentile Bellini: *Procession From St Mark's Square*, 1496, oil on canvas, 367,5 x 746 cm, Accademia, Venice

Campo Santa Margherita, one of the largest squares after the Piazza, until the 19th century functioned precisely as a *campo* – that is, an open space or arena – for the buying and selling of goods, and was reserved exclusively for the operations of merchants from outside the city. The square is surrounded by houses built in the 14th and 15th centuries. Today, it is a pleasantly sociable place with seats strategically placed beneath trees to give shade from the sun, and with a great number of cafés. There is an open-air market most mornings. This is the university district of Venice. At the end of the scholastic year students come here to celebrate their success.

On the Rio di San Barnaba, a floating market sells the fruit and vegetables that have come in fresh from the lagoon's islands.

To the south of Dorsoduro, and separated from it by the Canale della Giudecca, the 'island' of Giudecca is more accurately a collection of islets all very close to each other. Its elongatedly thin shape has earned it the nickname Spinalunga ('the long spine'). The derivation of its real name, Giudecca, remains controversial. Whatever the truth of the matter, it was a place reminiscent enough of the open countryside for wealthy Venetians to wish to use it as a retreat or resort. And today it remains an area that is particularly peaceful, much of the land taken up with growing fruits and vegetables for the city.

34. Statuary in the garden of the Guggenheim Museum
35. The pavement in the Salute
36. Giambattista Tiepolo: *Devotees in a Loggia*, fresco, 400 x 186 cm, Accademia, Venice
37. The Salute

In supplication to Christ the Redeemer that he might bring to a halt the spread of the horrifying plague epidemic of 1576, the Senate decided on the construction here of a church dedicated to The Redeemer. The architect chosen to design Il Redentore was Antonio Palladio (1508–80). The work was finished off by da Ponte in 1592.

On the east of the island stands the superbly appointed hotel, the Cipriani, which has a splendid swimming-pool. On the west, in stark contrast, stands the Mulino Stucky – an old red-brick flour-mill in neo-gothic style. Built at the end of the 19th century, its proprietor was murdered by one of his employees in 1910. The mill is currently being restored.

The island of San Giorgio Maggiore, east of the Giudecca, is directly opposite the Piazetta and the Doge's Palace. It formerly controlled the movement of all shipping into the lagoon from the open sea.

The church of San Giorgio Maggiore, near the north-western tip of the island, was begun by Palladio and finished off by Vincenzo Scamozzi. Built in white Istrian stone, it is quite blinding to look at on days of high sunshine. The panorama from the top of the bell-tower (*campanile*), which dates from the 18th century, includes exceptional views of San Marco, the Giudecca and the lagoon. At the foot of the campanile, the cloisters of the old Benedictine monastery have been perfectly restored and are well worth attention. Left abandoned and dilapidated when the Napoleonic troops pulled out, the monastery was taken over and transformed only in 1951 by the wealthy art patron Vittorio Cini. It is now run as a highly successful centre for international conventions on art and/or culture.

38. Part of the façade of the Palazzo Contarini
39. Inside the church of Santa Maria del Carmelo or dei Carmini
40. Gondolas alongside the Fondamente Zattere
41. A *Rio*

42

43

47. A view of the bell-tower of San Giorgio Maggiore above the cloisters, and of the Giudecca
48. The Giudecca
49. The cloisters of the monastery of San Giorgio Maggiore
50. Inside the church of San Giorgio Maggiore

SAN POLO AND SANTA CROCE

AFTER crossing the Rialto Bridge the visitor is confronted with the fruit and vegetable markets – the Erberia – and the fish market – the Pescheria – in the district of San Polo. The entire area around the bridge has always corresponded to the most important commercial and economic zone of the city. This is where the spice market was, and the market that bought and sold silks and precious stones... And this is also where the slave market used to be. At the peak of the city's trading eminence (13th to 15th centuries), it was here that the banks opened and flourished alongside newfangled insurance companies. Also doing good business were the prostitutes around Cassiano and the multitude of wine bars in the area. Today, the *filles de joie* have gone – but as in every great and scenic city, the sellers of souvenirs, food and drink for tourists have proliferated in their stead.

The area of Rialto was initially settled in something of a rush. To get from one side of the Canal Grande to the other at first meant transportation in either direction by ferry (*traghetto*), not only for goods but for people too. Then, to make life easier, a pontoon bridge was set up, followed in due course by a solid wooden bridge. That burned down many times over, and so in 1591 da Ponte had it reconstructed once and for all in Istrian stone. It was a single-arched span, was built at the very narrowest point of the Canal, and required more than 6,000 wooden piles to be driven into the bed of the waterway and the banks to support it. Small shops lined each side of the bridge.

On the San Marco side of the bridge, the Fondaco dei Tedeschi was the warehousing area for German (*Tedeschi*) merchants. On the San Polo side, the Palazzo dei Camerlenghi housed the Treasury department of the Republic.

51. The Rialto Bridge

San Polo is the smallest of Venice's *sestieri*, on the periphery of which lies the enormous Campo San Polo. It is a square that has an easy, familiar atmosphere, and it is the location for many cultural displays and open-air exhibitions.

On the Campo dei Frari stands the imposing if somewhat forbidding church of Santa Maria Gloriosa dei Frari (known to all simply as 'the Frari'). Built in red brick, lighter than marble, its style is gothic with an admixture of Byzantine and Roman elements. It was consecrated as a Franciscan foundation in 1492, and remains one of the two truly great churches in Venice – the other is the church of Santi Giovanni e Paolo in Castello.

52. The fruit and vegetable market – the Erberia
53. The fish market – the Pescheria
54. Rio San Giacomo dell' Orio

The interior of the church surprises a visitor with its richness. To one end, above the high altar, is the masterly *Assumption of the Virgin* by Titian (1518). The sacristy contains paintings in medieval Byzantine style by Veneziano (1334), other work by Vivarini, and a marvellous *Madonna and Child Enthroned With Saints* by Giovanni Bellini (triptych, 1488). Behind the 15th-century rood-screen 124 marquetry panels by Marco Cozzi (1468) decorate the choir stalls. The tombs of various doges are situated within the church, as is the tomb of the composer Monteverdi. The strange, pyramidal, neoclassical tomb of the sculptor Antonio Canova stands rather oddly next to the baroque monument (by Longhena) of Doge Giovanni Pesaro. Opposite it is the Renaissance tomb of Titian.

The ancient monastery of the Frari houses the official state archives of the city of Venice.

On the comparatively small Campo San Rocco, the church of San Rocco – built in the 18th century to replace a former church of the 16th century – harbours the relics of St Roch (Rocco). This holy man, born in Montpellier in 1295, is best known to Italians as the patron saint of plague-sufferers, and it was in an attempt to invoke his help and protection that Venice had his body transported there in 1485.

The foundation stone of the Scuola Grande di San Rocco was laid in 1478. Bartolomeo Bon (or Buon) took up work on it in 1515, and after his death a series of other architects contributed until it was completed in 1560.

The *scuole* (guilds, with their guildhalls) were characteristic of Venice from the 13th century on. Secular institutions, each nonetheless claimed a patron protector-saint. Their wealth stemmed partly from donations by rich aristocrats and well-to-do middle-class merchants, but much of it went directly on measures to care for the poor, the bereaved, the sick and the needy.

In the 15th century there were six Grandi Scuole (of which that of San Rocco was one) and close on 400 Minori Scuole. Not many of them had their own guild-hall, let alone their own church, but the wealthiest of those that had both tended to have them decorated by the most celebrated artists they could bring in. In addition to the power of wealth, however, the *scuole* carried a weight of social authority in the contemporary political life of the city. So much so that in 1806 Napoleon ordered them all to be closed down, and the works of art they held were for the most part taken over by the Accademia. Today, a mere three *scuole* continue to function in any real sense.

55. Campo San Polo
56. Titian: *The Assumption of the Virgin*, 1518
57. Giovanni Bellini (triptych): *Madonna and Child Enthroned With Saints*, 1488

It is thus to the Scuola Grande di San Rocco that the visitor who really wants to marvel at the immense talent of Tintoretto should go. An excellent example is to be found on the first floor, in the sala dell' Albergo – *The Crucifixion* (1565). Specialising in chiaroscuro, in vivid scenes, in intensity of coloration using a palette of particularly pure colours, Tintoretto brought considerable movement into his paintings. In his own life he was both liberal and passionate, preferring to work on a lifelong retainer rather than to be paid on commission for each work of art.

In the Great Hall, still on the first floor, the floor surface is of marble and the ceiling – covered in gilded panels – is as richly decorated as are the walls. All but lost in the midst of such splendour are two Tiepolos, two Titians and a Giorgione in individual supporting frames. The room is simply stupefying in the magnificence of what it contains.

Hidden behind the monastery of the Frari is the church and the Scuola di San Giovanni Evangelista. The *scuola* is one of the oldest in Venice. Concerts of classical music are popular there.

Santa Croce, on the other hand, is different. Bordered to the north by the Canal Grande and to the south by San Polo and Dorsoduro, its western side, it has to be said, has very little of any real interest.

There is no longer even an ecclesiastical establishment called Santa Croce – the monastery of that name was razed to the ground in the 19th century and replaced by the Giardino Papadopoli, a small green oasis of trees and grass.

To get to the Rialto having just arrived in Venice, the visitor can either board a *vaporetto* and take a trip down the Canal Grande or walk through the districts of Santa Croce and San Polo. The journey on foot is not easy for first-timers – it involves many twists and turns – but on or off the route there are some wonderful places to discover. Like, for instance, the Campo San Giacomo dell' Orio.

58. The church of San Rocco and the Scuola di San Giovanni Evangelista
59. On the first floor inside the Scuola di San Giovanni Evangelista
60. A well-head on the Campo San Giacomo dell' Orio
61. Campo Stin

CANNAREGIO

IN the south-west of Cannaregio, Santa Lucia central railway station was built in 1861, taking the name of the church that had once stood there. It is right next to the Canal Grande. The railway has linked Venice with the mainland since 1846, and the 'railway' bridge called the Ponte della Libertà (1933) has also enabled cars to drive at least as far as the gates of Venice before being left at the community car parks. What with the residents of Mestre and Marghera who commute to work in Venice and with the huge flux of tourists who are forever turning up in their thousands, this district tends to be crowded with people day and night.

For all that, it is significant that most of these people are generally on their way somewhere else, either by *vaporetto* or on foot.

During the 19th century, in order to make it easier for Venetians to travel around the city, it was decided to create a pedestrian thoroughfare linking the station with the Rialto. From Rio Terrà Lista di Spagna near the station across the Ponte delle Guglie right over to the Strada Nuova, the route also linked major commercial sites. For some of its length, the width of the new route is liable to astound today's visitor, especially if he or she has until then been walking down one of the *calli*. The thought springs unbidden to the mind that on such a roadway *cars* might safely be driven. Sacrilege!

On this invitingly broad thoroughfare stand two large department stores, Standa and Coin.

It is in this most peaceful of districts that the oldest Jewish community in European history is located. From the 11th century Jewish people lived on the islands south of Dorsoduro nicknamed Spinalunga but better known as the Giudecca. The Venetians were both tolerant of them and suspicious of them, and the Jews rather kept themselves to themselves.

62. The Ponte delle Guglie

By the 14th century, however, Jewish financiers had established commercial credit organisations both in Venice and on the mainland. This did not meet with universal approval, and one of the stipulations enforced by the League of Cambrai in 1509 was that Jews be restricted to Venice alone. The restriction was tightened further in 1516, when Jews were obliged to move to occupy an altogether much smaller area in the north of Cannaregio. It was a place known for the outflow of the water-stream used in the old metal-smelting works there, and was called 'the gusher' or 'jet' – in modern Italian *getto*, but in contemporary Venetian *ghetto* – and this is how that word derives in many other languages (including English) today.

A little later, in 1541, Jews hounded from Spain and Portugal made their home in the Ghetto Vecchio. More Jews, this time from the Levant (the Near East), arrived in the 17th century. The Scuola Spagnola and the Scuola Levantina have been in active operation ever since. Inside, the *scuole* are richly decorated by Venetian artists.

The area bounded by the Canale di Cannaregio and the Rio della Misericordia during those centuries was kept under very close observation. The Jews specialised in banking, in health care (they were renowned as skilled physicians) and in the production of ready-to-wear clothes. Even at this time, though, they had to have upon them, clearly visible, a yellow badge denoting their ethnicity.

The whole Ghetto was locked and barred from midnight to dawn, so that no one could enter or leave. All the windows that overlooked the Canale di Cannaregio were walled in. And as more and more Jews arrived, and elbowroom became even more restricted, the houses could only expand upwards. Some of them reached seven or eight storeys, towering over the narrow *calli* beneath. Nearly 5,000 people lived cramped up together on this one edge of the city – a city in which, despite their economic success, the Jews were not accorded the same rights as all the other citizens and were specifically excluded from political and social activity.

63. One of the narrow *calli*
64. A building in the Ghetto

65. The church of the Madonna dell' Orto
66. The Campo Sant' Alvise
67. The Rio San Felice

It was Napoleon Bonaparte who ordered the Ghetto to be opened up. Even then, the Jews at last attained their rightful status as citizens only when Venice finally became part of the Kingdom of Italy in 1866.

In this rather odd but strangely peaceful area to the north of Cannaregio, three *rii* which run parallel to the Canale di Cannaregio expedite the speedy passage of goods to and fro. On the Rio di Sant' Alvise, the church of that name (14th century) contains beautiful frescoes on its ceiling and some works by Tiepolo.

The church of the Madonna dell' Orto, built in gothic style, was decorated by Tintoretto who, at his death in 1594, was interred here. Within the church is his very impressive *The Last Judgement*, and opposite of it, his *The Adoration of the Golden Calf*. On the Fondamenta dei Mori stands what used to be Tintoretto's house.

The church of Santa Maria dei Miracoli, located on the border with neighbouring Castello and built by Lombardo at the end of the 15th century, is itself a little miracle. Its exterior has recently been greatly restored and now proudly exhibits quantities of marble in pastel shades. The inside is no less magical. Marco Polo's house is a mere stone's throw away, in the Corte Seconda del Milion.

Still in Cannaregio, the Fondamenta Nuove starts at the Sacca della Misericordia and runs as far as the city hospital, which is in the district of Castello. Its quiet quaysides, all facing out northwards, look nothing like those of the Zattere in Dorsoduro. Dating from the 16th century, they are distinctly uninviting in the evenings, but at the end of the afternoons the contrast is captivating, showing the offshore islands of San Michele (the burial ground of Venice) and, behind it, Murano, in a really fine light. Ferries to the islands are available from the quay on the Fondamenta Nuove.

68. The church of the Abazia
69. Cannaregio at night

CASTELLO

THIS *sestieri* of Venice is the largest and the most diverse. It also contains the most surprises – for those who look for them. Castello comprises the part of Venice immediately to the east of San Marco and Cannaregio. In the south, separated from the Doge's Palace by the Rio di Palazzo, it is often crowded with tourists, who naturally flock there straight from San Marco. From the Molo (the quayside in front of the Piazza), the Riva degli Schiavoni leads on to other quaysides that run the length of the district all the way to the public gardens.

This Riva is always full of tourists because it is from here that boats and ferries depart for the Lido and San Giorgio. It is the quayside to which, in former centuries, ships from the Dalmatian coast used to bring their merchandise for sale, including slaves. That is how the Riva got its name: *schiavoni* is the Italian for 'slavers'.

The church of Santa Maria della Visitazione (better known as the Pietà) is Vivaldi's church. The Ospedale della Pietà (15th century) took in girl-children who had been abandoned and gave them a good musical education, and Antonio Vivaldi (1687–1741) was their teacher. A gifted violinist, he was at the same time a prodigious composer, particularly of concertos. Orchestral concerts given in the chapel by the girls of the Ospedale with Vivaldi as conductor were both popular and fashionable. The Ospedale church was built in 1706 by Giorgio Massari, and decorated by Tiepolo.

Not far away, the church of San Zaccaria displays a Renaissance façade designed by the architect Codussi. Inside, among other gems, is a beautiful retable (altar shelf) by Giovanni Bellini (1505). The adjoining convent accepted only the daughters of the wealthiest residents of Venice – and was renowned for gaiety and licence!

70. The Riva degli Schiavoni

The Scuola San Giorgio degli Schiavoni was founded in 1451, and decorated by Carpaccio. At around the same time, Greek residents of Venice – of which the number had increased considerably following the fall of Constantinople to the Turks in 1453 – built themselves a *scuola* and a church. The church's interior displays Byzantine art in all its richness.

To the north of Castello, the Fondamenta Nuove runs close by the Ospedale Civile, the municipal hospital, which replaced the Scuola Grande di San Marco during the Napoleonic period. The entrance to the old *scuola* leads on to the enormous Campo Santi Giovanni e Paolo – called San Zanipolo by the locals – next to the church of the same name. This church, in red brick and in the Gothic Venetian style, is the largest church in Venice. It was built by the Dominicans between the 13th and 15th centuries, and has welcomed many a Doge to his final resting-place within.

The statue to the right of the entrance to the church is that of *Condottiere* Bartolomeo Colleoni, sculpted by Andrea Verrochio in 1488. Colleoni amassed a considerable fortune, which he then wished to bequeath to the city on condition that some form of memorial to him be performed each day in the Piazza. It was a proposition that was not acceptable to the authorities of the Republic – so they placed his statue instead beside the Scuola Grande di San Marco so that, in a sort of diplomatic gesture not untypical of Venetians, he was seen daily by 'San Marco' even if it was not the San Marco he had intended.

The Campo Santi Giovanni e Paolo is a great place to spend a moment of relaxation, for it is both tranquil and full of liveliness.

Across from the French Library, the Ospedaletto is one of the four large hospitals in Venice established to care for the elderly and the destitute. Musical concerts used to

71. Windows overlooking the Rio dei Greci
72. The Rio dei Greci

73. The Rio dei Greci
74. Campo Santi Giovanni e Paolo and the church

be given here, and its Sala della Musica (1776–77), recently restored, is a real gem. The murals are by Jacopo Guarana, with *trompe-l'oeil* effects by Agostino Mengozzi Colonna.

Even if The Arsenal today is no longer a military zone from which all civilians are excluded, it is worthy of note because of its glorious past. Founded in 1104, The Arsenal was Venice's naval supply dockyard, closely concerned with the maritime dominance of the Republic

from the end of the 12th century. At one stage it was the largest naval supply dockyard in the world, and the most efficient, for the *arsenalotti* were highly specialist workers. Just before the Battle of Lepanto (1571), for example, The Arsenal managed to completely equip around 100 galleys in a matter of 50 days.

Its activity declined after the time of Napoleon. Now all it does is passively receive the admiration of the tourists who gawp at the Renaissance entrance (1460) –

75. *Condottiere* Bartolomeo Colleoni
76. View of the canals

which is flanked on each side by a marble lion brought from Greece in the 17th century – and who see only a small area of The Arsenal as they take their *motoscafo* circular tour of the city.

Part of The Arsenal, in any case, has been occupied by the Biennale for a couple of years, and it is to be hoped that some positive decisions will be taken about its future sometime soon.

Once known as Olivolo, the island of San Pietro di Castello has been inhabited since very early times. It was the castle that once stood on this island that gave its name – Castello – to the whole district. Here, too, was the site of Venice's cathedral until 1807, when that title was formally transferred to the basilica of San Marco. The ex-cathedral church is thus one of the oldest churches in Venice (7th century), in white Istrian stone and with a façade designed by Palladio himself.

77. Front door of the Arsenal
78. San Pietro di Castello

THE CANAL GRANDE AND ITS PALAZZI

THE Canal Grande (Grand Canal) or Canalazzo – a merging of *canal* and *palazzo* – on a map looks like a capital S backwards. It cuts the city in two for a length of around 2.5 miles (4 kilometres) and has many *palazzi* on both banks.

Between the Piazzale Roma and the Bacino San Marco, this primary route within the city is spanned by a mere three bridges: the Scalzi, the Rialto, and the Accademia. The only other way of getting across the Canal Grande is to take one of the *traghetti*.

In former times, goods transported by ship to the city arrived via the Canal Grande at the large warehouses that served also as dwellings. Just as in English, this is how the name of the warehouse became also the name of the proprietorial family that lived on the premises, in the form 'the House of' someone. In Italian, 'House' is *Casa*; in Venetian, it got shortened to simply *Ca'*.

The warehouses in the very early times were quite small. But as trade expanded and the merchants became rich, what had been just warehouses with rooms to sleep in were enlarged and sumptuously decorated so that they became the veritable palaces – *palazzi* – we admire today.

Merchandise was unloaded by the main goods entrance (which was marked out by a floating landing-stage with flagpoles displaying the family colours) and then stored on ground level. A mezzanine floor between the ground and first floors housed the offices. And on the first floor, or *pianonobile*, was the largest room, the spectacularly ornate great chamber or *portego*, from which smaller rooms branched out in all directions.

79. One of the *traghetti*

The Canal Grande features many luxurious *palazzi* separated by more modest dwellings, creating a panoply of different styles that nonetheless harmonise graciously together. A good number of *palazzi* have of course already gone for ever, but enough remain to be able to spot the styles of different eras. At the entry to the Canale di Cannaregio, the Palazzo Labia – built in baroque style – is now the headquarters of the radio and TV service RAI. Inside it are some excellent murals by Tiepolo. Opposite San Marcuola is one of the most important *palazzi* on the Canal Grande: the Fondaco dei Turchi. In Venetian-Byzantine style, flanked by two turrets and well disposed for trading by water, it was hired out to Turkish merchants in the 17th century. Badly restored during the 19th century, today it houses the city's museum of natural history. Next to San Marcuola, the Palazzo Loredan-Vendramin-Calergi (begun in the 16th century) has belonged to the city since 1946, and is the winter casino.

80. The Canal Grande
81. The Fondaco dei Turchi
82. The Ca' d'Oro

Ca' Pesaro, built in baroque style during the 17th century by Baldassare Longhena, is now the site of the museum of modern art and the oriental museum.

One of the most beautiful Gothic *palazzi* in Venice is the Ca' d'Oro. Built in the 15th century by Matteo Raverti, it is without doubt the most celebrated *palazzo* on the Canal Grande, if not in the whole of Venice – apart, of course, from the Doge's Palace. Following unconscionable alterations to it made at the whim of a Russian lady dancer, Baron Giorgio Franchetti bought the Ca' d'Oro at the end of the 19th century and had it superbly restored. On his death he bequeathed the *palazzo* and the contents he had put into it to the city, which turned it into a fascinating museum.

In the Rialto, the Fondaco dei Tedeschi, built in the 16th century and today the central post office, was once a storehouse hired out to German merchants.

The Gothic Palazzo Pisani-Moretta has much to recommend inside it, notably paintings by Veronese, by Tiepolo and by Piazzetta. To be able to afford its upkeep, its proprietors rent it out for private or public occasions (receptions, dances, publicity events, and so forth). Connected with this *palazzo*, the Barbarigo della Terrazza overlooks the Rio San Polo. Unfortunately for Venice, its once remarkable collection of works of art now graces the Hermitage Museum in St Petersburg.

The Ca' Foscari, on the second curve of the Canal Grande, was constructed by Bartolomeo Bon in the mid-15th century for Doge Francesco Foscari. Bought up by the city in the 19th century, it is now the principal seat of the University of Venice.

83. One end of the Canal Grande
84. Giandomenico Tiepolo: *Pulcinella's swing*,
    1791?, Ca' Rezzonico, Venice
85. The Palazzo Pisani-Moretta

86. The Ca' Dario
87. *Gondolieri*
88. A gondola and its *ferro*

The Palazzo Grassi, built by Giorgio Massari for the Grassi family at the beginning of the 18th century, is currently the property of the Fiat Foundation. It was the last of the great *palazzi* to be constructed on the Canal Grande.

The Ca' Rezzonico was begun in 1667 by Longhena and completed later by Massari on behalf of the Rezzonico family. Under restoration, it is Venice's museum of the 18th century and contains frecoes by Tiepolo *père* and *fils* and by Guarana, and paintings by Canaletto, Longhi and Guardi.

Not far away is the superb Renaissance *palazzo* the Ca' d'Oro, which has a charm all of its own and receives attention accordingly. Its asymmetric façade is covered in multicoloured marble discs. Look at it carefully, for there is something macabre about this building – its owners tend to die in violent and often bizarre fashion.

Of course the Canal Grande no longer exhibits the same sort of mercantile activity that it did in the Middle Ages, nor indeed the activity concerned with the more genteel customs of the 18th century. But there is still one form of craft that from those times to this has plied the same water for a living – the gondola.

89

89. *La Serenata*
90. The entrance to a *palazzo*

In former centuries the gondola was the main means of transport for people and goods all over the city, doing much of what today is instead done by the *traghetto*. By the end of the 11th century, aristocratic Venetian families each employed their own gondolier – perhaps more than one. The gondoliers in due course formed themselves into something of a closed circle: woe betide any who divulged their confidences and their trade secrets. Asymmetrical in shape, and black all over following the laws passed during the 16th century against any form of ostentation, the gondola is tricky to handle and requires a lengthy apprenticeship. On the prow, or *ferro*, are six 'teeth', representing the six districts of Venice, and above them the Doge's cap of office.

There are certain sites popular with tourists where convoys of gondolas – occasionally accompanied by a musical ensemble – are arranged as a special feature. Unlike the *vaporetti* and the water-taxis with which they have competed since the 19th century, the gondolas have little effect in the displacement or erosion of the foundations of the buildings they pass. They do not cause such a backwash which regularly exposes to the corrupting air the piles which must at all times remain submerged if they are not to rot away.

FESTIVALS IN VENICE

VENETIANS love their traditional feast days and festivals, and regard it as a duty to celebrate them with due fervency. Nonetheless, although the Venice Carnival reached its peak during the 18th century, it came to an abrupt halt in 1797 on the fall of the Republic. Twenty years ago, however, the Venetians finally took up where they had left off, resuming it in 18th-century style. Today, the Carnival lasts for two weeks, although it still ends on the evening of Mardi Gras (Shrove Tuesday). Mind you, in the 18th century it might go on for as long as six months, with a few minor interruptions. In their costumes – but even more specifically, in their masks – the Venetians could mingle with each other without any connotations of social rank.

Throughout Europe, Venice became a city renowned for its licence, its pleasures and its debauchery. It was all too easy! Wearing a mask allowed anyone to get away with anything. No wonder Casanova – that learned libertine, gambler and lecher – was able to throw himself whole-heartedly into enjoying such a semi-permanent atmosphere of abandoned festivity.

Casanova rather symbolises this Venice *en fête*. Condemned to imprisonment by the religious authorities of the Republic, he found himself immured within the dungeons of the Doge's Palace, but escaped several months later. His *Memoirs* describe his celebrated breakout from the Leads in 1756. On his eventual return to Venice, it was – almost unbelievably – as a secret agent on behalf of those selfsame religious authorities!

And it has to be said that this century of festivity, of gambling and of licentiousness was also the century in which theatre, music and colour came into their own.

91. Fireworks over the Bacino San Marco

The dramatist Carlo Goldoni killed off the traditional *commedia dell' arte* with its stock characters. In favour of improvisation, he instituted the Comedy of Manners which was at one and the same time more realistic and more cruel.

In painting, this was the time in which Tiepolo executed his marvellous frescoes, in which Canaletto and Guardi produced their *vedute*, and in which Longhi contributed his innovatory *genre* scenes of everyday life.

The century of such spectacular wealth and enjoyment was followed by one of abject poverty. 'Tomorrow' had caught up, with a vengeance.

On Ascension Day every year, Venice celebrates the anniversary of its 'marriage' with the sea. It is the *Festa della Sensa*, and it commemorates an event that took place a thousand years ago following a successful expedition to chastise the inhabitants of troublesome Dalmatia. In Venice's barge of state, the *Bucentaure*, the contemporary Doge processed to San Nicolo del Lido accompanied by a flotilla of lesser craft. At the harbour mouth, the Doge took from his hand a golden ring

presented to him by the pope and flung it into the water, crying 'With this ring we thee wed, O sea, in token of the true and perfect partnership'.

The Sunday following Ascension Day has recently become the date for a highly popular regatta (the *Vogalonga*) that sees races take place across the lagoon.

Every year Venice renews its gratitude to Christ the Redeemer for putting an end to the plague epidemic in 1576. It does so with the *Festa del Redentore*. On the third Sunday in July a temporary bridge of boats links the Fondamente Zattere with the church of Il Redentore, across which the Venetians – and any tourists who have the stomach for it – make their way to the Giudecca. It is not just those who dislike crowds who would do well to stay clear, for the main purpose is to eat either on the Fondamente on the Giudecca side or on the decorated boats as they float in the Bacino San Marco, or *on both*. To round it all off, there is a firework display enough to enthuse even the most blasé. Tradition demands that Venetians go on partying on the Lido until dawn.

The *Regata Storica* takes place on the Canal Grande on the first Sunday in September, when the waterway comes alive with a veritable cavalcade of craft. They parade in teams, while a model of the *Bucentaure* floats gently in the current.

The Venetians fulfil a vow on 21 November each year – a vow that celebrates continued health, and that commemorates the end of the plague epidemic of 1630 and so goes back to the foundation of the church of the Salute. A bridge of boats this time links the district of San Marco with the Salute.

94

92–95. Masks and costumes

95

Although not really anything to do with festivals, two other important cultural events take place annually in Venice. The Mostra (the 'Show'), or international film festival, begins in the first week of September. Based on the Lido, it has been going since August 1932. And the Biennale exhibition of contemporary art unfolds every two years in the Giardini Pubblici, at Sant' Elena and in part of The Arsenal. This exhibition was inaugurated as far back as in April 1895, and is now regarded as both successful and prestigious. Artists who don't make selection for the exhibition may nonetheless display their works elsewhere in the city.

96. The Regatta
97. The Regatta: the women's team
98. The Regatta: the men's team

THE ISLANDS AND THE LAGOON

VENICE is essentially a collection of little islands situated at the centre of a sea-lagoon some 32 miles (50 kilometres) long and nearly 9.5 miles (15 kilometres) wide. A great number of other islets surround it, some of them inhabited, some not.

To the east of the city, a coastal bar just offshore protects Venice from the Adriatic Sea. It is in three parts. One of them, the Lido de Venezia – ordinarily known simply as the Lido (which is where the word comes from in English) – is a sandbank 7.5 miles (12 kilometres) long by about six-tenths of a mile (1 kilometre) wide. A place of solitude for centuries, it is the site of a Jewish cemetery in which some of the tombs date from as far back as the 1200s.

It was not until the mid-19th century that the area was transformed into a popular watering-place, when the Albergo del Bagno – made famous by its appearance in Luchino Visconti's film *Death in Venice* – was built. The modern traffic and luxurious houses with large gardens now seem far removed from the ambience in the ancient centre of the city.

99. The 'Hotel des Bains' on the Lido
100. The Lido

One of the major islands, San Michele, can be seen from the Fondamenta Nuove, San Cristoforo being linked to it. After Napoleon forbade interments in the central part of the city, burials have ever since taken place here.

A little bit further off is the isle of Murano, which was one of the first to suffer a population explosion when all the artisans in glass were obliged to leave the centre of Venice by official civic order 'for reasons of security' at the end of the 18th century. Artistic creativity remains important here. The basilica of Santi Maria e Donato, first built in the 7th century and reconstructed during the 12th, is Venetian-Byzantine with its apsidal mosaics in gold, its icons and its (12th-century) pavement.

Further into the lagoon, Burano is a village of fisher-folk known primarily for its lacework. The houses on this island are all painted in different colours, a characteristic that attracts huge numbers of artists and writers.

101. The basilica of Santi Maria e Donato on Murano
102. The cinema on the Lido
103. Brightly-coloured house frontages on Burano
104–105. Glass-blowing on Murano

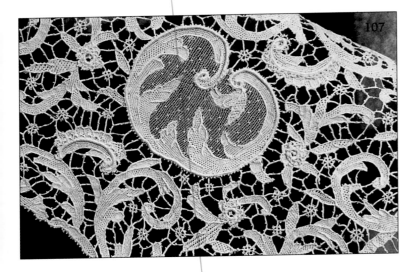

Torcello, today all but deserted, was at one time the most populous island in the lagoon. Those who fled Altino at the advance of the barbarians in the 7th century took up residence on this island despite the fact that – or perhaps because – it was swampy and generally inhospitable an economically viable and even significant culture eventually flourished there. But it all came to nothing in the 14th century.

The Byzantine cathedral of Santa Maria Assunta on Torcello is one of the oldest churches in the lagoon (built in the 7th century). It was restyled during the 10th and 11th centuries. From the outside the brick exterior gives little indication of the richness and beauty inside the building, for a visitor who steps into the cathedral is at once overwhelmed by the golden quality of the light streaming all around. The effect stems from the top of the apse, where there is a Virgin and Child with a golden base, dating from the 13th century, together with other mosaics. Down below, a tessellated *Last Judgement* gives an all-too-realistic vision of the dreadful punishments in store for sinners. A portico links the cathedral with the church of Santa Fosca, built in Byzantine style in the 12th century.

Several other islands that are less well known (San Lazzaro degli Armeni, San Francesco del Deserto, and others) still have communities of one size or another on them. Each island tends to be a focus for a single way of life: a monastic foundation, a kitchen garden, a prison, a psychiatric hospital, and so on.

Venice occupies part of a lagoon. But the lagoon is itself the result of a comparatively recent geological phenomenon, going back only to the last Ice Age and the retreat of the alpine glaciers. Glacial rivers flowing down and across the plain of (what is now) the Po brought with them the alluvial silt that then caused the formation

of the coastal strip now protecting the islands of the lagoon from the rigours of the Adriatic.

The water of the lagoon is brackish. Its salinity decreases from east to west, thanks to the constant ebb and flow of the tide through the three gaps between the three *lidi*.

106. Burano
107–108. Burano lacework
109. Street sign

110

110. The island of Torcello in the middle of
     the lagoon.
111. The church of Santa Fosca and the
     cathedral of Santa Maria Assunta
112. Inside the cathedral

A lagoon is not generally a permanent feature but naturally evolves towards its own extinction. Erosion by the sea of the sandbanks that contain it, and silting up by alluvial deposits from the inland waterways that flow into it both tend toward a lagoon's becoming choked with brackish mud. It becomes an unhealthy malarial swamp. Nonetheless, humans do go to such places and live by catching fish and extracting salt. They may set up small communities in rickety shacks. But to have succeeded in creating a magnificent city on such unpromising terrain must count as something approaching a miracle – even if plain ignorance might have contributed at the beginning. Such a miracle does demonstrate the determination of the human spirit, at least.

The first inhabitants of the lagoon put up with the changes in the flow of the rivers and the height of the tides, and refused to be discouraged from setting up home there. Venetians thereafter consequently battled for centuries, for millennia, to maintain their foothold on their precarious pitch. They diverted the watercourses of rivers, constructed *murazzi* – sea walls – in Istrian stone on the *lidi*, and built dikes at various levels in order to prevent either the silting up or the drying out of the marshes. By preventing the lagoon's natural evolution in this way, they preserved the city.

The end of the Republic (in 1796) also saw the end of all the great engineering efforts on the lagoon.

In 1846, Venice lost its privileged position as primary island in the lagoon: it was linked to the mainland by a rail bridge just over 2 miles (3.5 kilometres) long. Then, specifically because of its geographical location, the area just across from it on the mainland was selected for unlimited industrial development. During the 20th century, vast industrial zones were therefore set up at Porto Marghera and Mestre. Marco Polo Airport was built – and required the draining of no less than one quarter of the entire lagoon. The water left could not flow away normally. Dredging and oil pollution on a grand scale befouled the water even more. The pumping out of underground water reservoirs and the extraction of natural gas further increased the rate of soil subsidence.

Tidal flooding (or *acque alte*) has always been a threat. But it has become more frequent, and the inundation has seriously weakened the basement floors of the buildings. The flood of 4 November 1966 submerged the Piazza to a depth of 4 feet (1.2 metres). Why did it happen? Subsidence, yes, but also a severely directional tide, the significant strength of the sirocco (the seasonal wind from the south), a low-pressure atmospheric system, water levels already high because of unusual amounts of rain, strong currents in the canals themselves because of reconstruction work involving artificial channels, the reduced overall capacity of the lagoon – all these contributory elements caused the lagoon to overflow… and Venice had its first experience of drowning.

113

The whole world reacted in surprise and panic, suddenly aware of how vulnerable Venice was.

International funding was made available and, under the aegis of UNESCO, restoration work was put in hand at least to refurbish the *palazzi* and do what could be done for individual works of art. However, the most important thing was to try to put a stop to the subsidence. All the artesian wells were closed down, and the extraction of natural gas was abruptly terminated. The next stage in the development of Porto Marghera was suspended indefinitely, and the activity of the industrial complex was reduced so that, for example, all oil-related enterprises remained at levels they had reached at the beginning of the 1990s. In spite of some damaging setbacks and the effects of natural subsidence, the overall loss of sedimentary undersoil has genuinely slowed since 1975.

Moreover, the restoration work went hand in hand with efforts to reduce the amount of pollution measured in the lagoon – pollution that stemmed from a city in which anything and everything went into the drains and thence the canals; from canals that had not been decontaminated for many decades; from factories and workshops that had been accustomed to using the lagoon for waste-disposal; from agricultural farms tending to use nitrate fertilisers which then leached into the waters and gave rise to abnormal 'blooms' of algae; from an atmosphere in which tonnes of sulphuric acid were suspended and might fall at any time on the city…. All these forms of pollution, which were putting Venice – the pearl of the lagoon – in such desperate jeopardy, were the work of humankind. The only factors contributory to erosion that had little or nothing to do with humans were the humidity and the saltiness of the air.

Further measures taken following the reduction of industrial activities at Porto Marghera have included the reinforcing of the *murazzi* along the coastal strip, the cleaning up of the canals, the total prohibition of the use of nitrate fertilisers, and the dispersal of the algal blooms. And at last the Venetians are taking precautions against the possibility of another *acqua alta*. A project involving locks and sluice-gates – Project MOSE – has been under serious consideration for some 20 years or so…

The last 100 years have been perilous for Venice. One can only hope that the warning has been well and truly taken to heart.

113. Inside the cathedral Santa Maria Assunta
114–115. *The Last Judgement* (details)

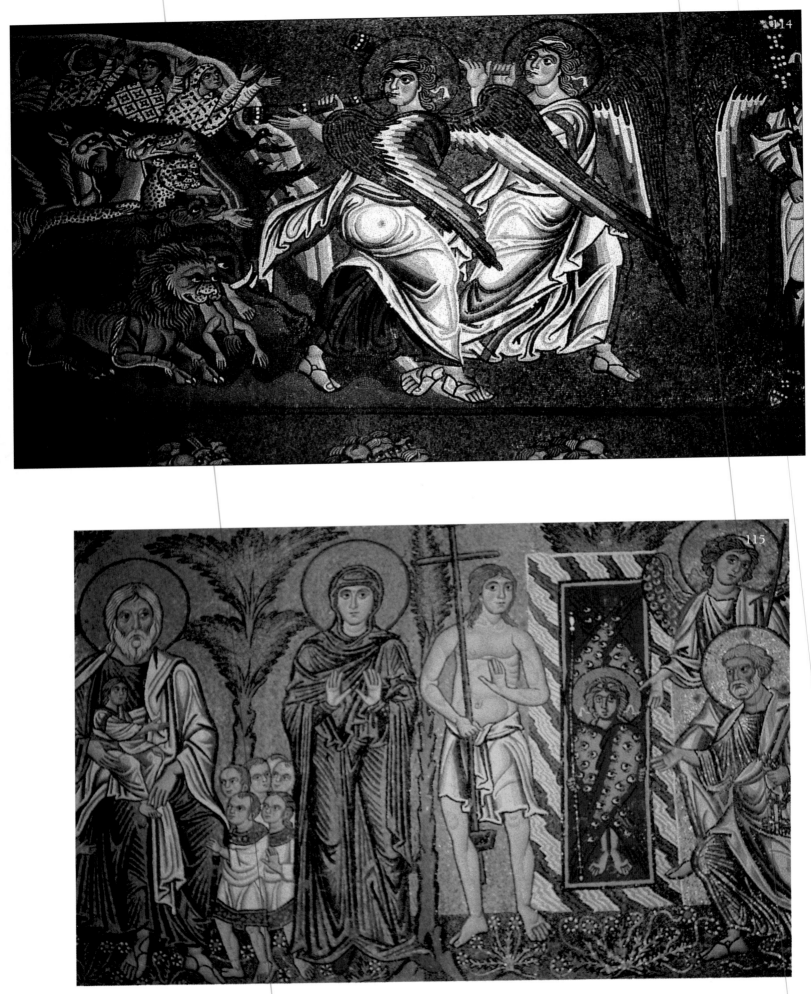

116

CONCLUSION

To be sure, Venice has encountered some difficult problems. Over the years it has lost a good proportion of its population – the city boasts no more than 70,000 residents today – while nonetheless having to accommodate a vast number of tourists. But it remains a city in which it is quite possible to lead a normal sort of life.

Venice is a gigantic pedestrian zone, and it is easy enough to get to where you want to go, and fast. It is a city on a human scale, and its inhabitants are not under the same types of stress as people are in London, New York or Paris.

It is a privilege to be able to live there, for its little inconveniences pale beside its quality of life and the beauty to be experienced in each instant.

The ghosts of the Doges are watching over the *Serenissima*…

116. The church of Santa Maria della Salute ('the Salute') at sunset

Publishing Director: Jean-Paul Manzo

Text: Véronique Laflèche

Layout: Albéric Girard & Cédric Pontes

Cover: Cédric Pontes

Publishing Assistant: Séverine Corson

Photographs: Andréa Luppi & Klaus H. Carl
Thanks also to the Italian Tourist Office in Venice
for their contribution of photos

Parkstone Press Ltd
Printed and bound in Singapore
ISBN 1 85995 765 X